TO DO OR NOT TO DO

HOW SUCCESSFUL LEADERS MAKE BETTER DECISIONS

GARY WINTERS

ERIK KLEIN

CONTENTS

HOW SUCCESSFUL LEADERS MAKE BETTER DECISIONS

By Gary Winters and Eric Klein

Web: www.garywinters.com
Email: gary@garywinters.com
Phone: 619-840-0148

Web: http://themindfulteam.com
Email: eric@dharmaconsulting.com
Phone: (760) 436-5535

To my daughters, Lyndsey and Hallie,
within whom the spirit of leadership burns brightly.

Gary Winters

To my wonderful wife, Deborah,
and my beautiful sons, Nathaniel and Aaron.
May we continue to learn, grow, and create together.

Eric Klein

EFFECTIVE LEADERS TAILOR THEIR DECISION-making style to the unique needs of the situation. *To Do or Not To Do* gives managers a practical process for using the right style at the right time. I wouldn't just recommend reading this book, I would recommend sharing it with team members!

Your next leadership decision should be to buy this book, read it, apply what you learn, and share it with your team!

Marshall Goldsmith
Author of *The Leader of the Future*. "America's preeminent coach" – Fast Company

To Do or Not To Do is sure to help all leaders make better decisions. Don't miss it!

Ken Blanchard
Coauthor of *The One Minute Manager*® and *The Secret*

For any manager who has been searching for the fundamental, simple truths behind the leadership challenge—control, power, accountability, commitment—Winters and Klein have captured their essence and spun them through a storytelling style that is both engaging and powerful. Here are real tools that can be applied today in a memorable and immediately productive way.

Joan Waltman
Vice President Engineering, QWBS, Qualcomm

To Do or Not To Do takes the mystery and guesswork out of one of management's most consistent dilemmas—when and how to involve others in decision making. The style and setting of the story provide for a fun, quick read and an easily remembered set of useful guidelines.

Denny Stone

Director, Service Innovation
Computer Sciences Corporation
GTS World Source Division

This quick-read parable lies in a sweet spot between Blanchard and Drucker—engaging storytelling that is also sufficiently prescriptive to give leaders direct guidance on handling real-world situations. All good managers want to empower their people, but it's never easy to know just when to share power, and when to pull it back. This book shows you how. It deserves a place both on the reference shelf and in the briefcase.

Greg McQuerter
CEO, The McQuerter Group

Entertaining and practical! In *To Do or Not To Do*, Winters and Klein clearly link the how and the why of making decisions to vital leadership issues like folly and wisdom, power and influence, control and vulnerability. Using pitch-perfect metaphors and dialogue, the authors' re-creation of King Solomon as super coach to a 21st Century manager provides a fresh approach for learning. If you are willing to take some risks to develop team skills, this book will illuminate your path.

Matt Ferrero
Team Leader, Center for Leadership Development
Internal Revenue Service

A delightful book about how leaders engage people to make better decisions. Gary Winters and Eric Klein have made this dimension of leadership easy to understand, and simple to execute. A "must-read" for anyone with the desire to lead their team to deeper engagement and better outcomes.

Deb Giampoli
Senior Director, Global Cohort Marketing
Kraft Foods

If you want people in your enterprise to be more engaged, connected, and creative, apply the principles of To Do or Not To Do. This deceptively simple book appears to be a straightforward, behaviorist's guide to leadership decision making. It is actually a guide to the kinds of conversations and agreements that would be a huge help to all parts of our troubled world. I hope this is just the first of many offerings from King Solomon's Wisdom School.

Jim Stuart
Teacher, Founding Executive Director of The Florida Aquarium

I love the book. It is practical, witty, and profound. The wisdom of *To Do or Not To Do* can be applied immediately to work (and other life) situations.

Jim Farris
President, James C. Farris & Associates

To Do or Not To Do is for enlightened leaders who know that involving employees in problem solving is key to improving the quality and acceptance of solutions. This book reveals how and when to do so.

William Kirkwood, PhD
Associate Dean of Special Programs and Professor of Communication
East Tennessee State University

This is as good as it gets for the busy leader who

needs both higher-minded wisdom and nitty-gritty results. This engaging story functions like a leadership seminar you can digest over a lunch hour. It will challenge you with provocative questions and equip you with pragmatic tools for cultivating high-performance teams.

Keep this one handy as a refresher anytime you need to make a decision and achieve and optimal results (i.e. every day).

Marian Baker, CPCC, PCC
A Top 50 Coach featured in "Profiles in Coaching; Best Practices in Leadership Coaching."

I'm not running a corporation and never will, but I do have a position of leadership with teams of volunteers, so I was very intrigued with how simple the process of decision-making can be. Using a "parable" format to explain the principles is wonderfully clever! The questions I might have asked were imbedded right into the story and I came away thinking even I can do this!

Betsy Virnelson
Parish Nurse, Mayfield Church

There is a great chasm between compliance and

commitment. Leaders can demand compliance but they must engage hearts and minds in order to gain commitment. This wise book provides a simple guide to help you understand how to effectively elicit the appropriate level of commitment needed on any decision.

Joyce Wycoff
Co-founder, InnovationNetwork

An excellent book for new first line supervisors (and their managers who should know this stuff but don't always practice it). Emphasizes there is definitely more than one effective way to approach supervisory tasks and that the best ways often engage and enroll their whole unit. The message to new supervisors is you don't have to be a "my way or the highway" type boss to be effective and respected by your employees.

Gill D. Park, Ph. D.
Principal, New Millennium Group

A very practical book to help managers decide how to make decisions. I've already integrated the terminology into my conversations and the concepts into my decision making.

Susan K. Gerke

Author of *Quick Guide to Interaction Styles and Working Remotely*

Winters and Klein present here through an unusual allegory a useful model for deciding how to make decisions about participative decision making. Managers who wrestle with how much to include others in their decision making should find this a quick and useful overview of how to approach this problem.

James G. Clawson

Darden Graduate School of Business Administration

University of Virginia

WHEN I FIRST LEARNED THAT Eric Klein and Gary Winters were going to write a book on what they teach about decision-making for leaders I was delighted. After all, these two had been coaching the leadership team in my organization and me for some time, and I've been quite pleased with the results. I knew immediately that the project would be invaluable for leaders in all walks of life. These two have a talent for making the complex simple, and they've mastered the timeless art of story-telling as a teaching method.

Most folks who have achieved a position of leadership have gotten there by the activism, follow-through and technical skills they have expressed so well early in their careers. That these can-do, take-charge folks rise to positions of increasing responsibility is not unexpected – even to them.

What may surprise them is that the skill sets that served so well in the past are not enough in their expanding role as a leader. Some, in an attempt to avoid micro-managing or interfering, will be tempted to disengage and simply delegate downward. Others will maintain their old behaviors and drive their people crazy by controlling and meddling. The middle ground, what I call shared leadership, is where effective leaders hold and share the power of decision making.

If you're in a leadership role, you'll find in this book a straightforward and sensible approach to decision-making that will enable you to bring out the best in your people while you remain fully engaged.

More than simply delegating downward, the effective leader employs a wide range of decision-making styles that challenge their people and themselves. Eric and Gary take the reader through an imaginary Wisdom School with King Solomon who employs the Socratic method to engage his student on leadership and decision-making.

What results is an easy-to-read guidebook that describes five decision-making styles and when they can be best employed. The text is fresh and compelling. The major points can be returned to again and again to refresh your memory. Effective leadership is not easy. Eric and Gary give the reader a fighting chance to getting it right.

I'm quite pleased to recommend this book, whole-heartedly and without reservation, to anyone in a leadership role.

Blake Anderson
General Manager
Orange County Sanitation District
Fountain Valley, California

INTRODUCTION

THIS IS THE STORY OF Alan, a fairly new and very busy manager in a large organization, whose To Do list is weighing heavily on his mind. Like leaders in all walks of life, Alan is responsible for making critical decisions. His *To Do* list is brimming with issues—some quite important, some not so important. Regardless, it's almost overwhelming.

Alan knows he should involve his people in the decision-making process, not only because it will lighten his own load but because involving more than one brain should lead to higher-quality decisions. Nonetheless, he's unsure how to proceed.

Our depiction of Alan is inspired by a participant at a management academy we facilitated several years ago. One afternoon, this new manager raised his hand and asked, "How can I get my people *to feel as though* they are involved in the decision-making process?" (our emphasis).

We gave him the benefit of the doubt, knowing that his question was sincere: he wanted techniques to include his staff in decisions. But we were struck by those three words: "feel as though." His question illustrates a dilemma shared by so many leaders, although it might be more accurate to say it like this: "How can I convince my people that they are helping me make critical decisions without my actually taking the risk of letting them make any?"

That's the rub, after all.

When you involve people in making decisions, some of their ideas will be different from yours, resulting in a decision that's different than you would have made without their input.

In theory, that's fine. In the real world, there might a problem: as the leader, you're still held accountable for those decisions.

Our workshop participant explained that he could see no good way to empower his staff without sacrificing his own authority and sense of control. He felt conflicted between his concerns about being held accountable for high-quality decisions and his desire to involve his staff in the process. In his view, since he was in charge, he should be making all the important decisions, yet he knew in his heart that his staff should participate. He simply didn't know how to reconcile these two beliefs.

Over the past twenty years or so, a lot has changed in our collective understanding of how effective organizational leaders lead. Much has been written about how good managers excel at listening, offering feedback, coaching others, and building productive teams. Concepts such as empowerment and employee involvement now permeate the literature and are the subject of countless leadership retreats. In some organizations, even conventional labels are changing—from boss to coach, from supervisor to team leader, for example. But changing labels isn't enough.

Agreeing that it's important to involve people in decision making is different from knowing how. Or when, for that matter. After all, decisions run the gamut from the trivial to the consequential, and few would argue that everyone on the team should be involved in every decision. What Alan needs—what every leader needs—is a simple system to wisely and effectively involve people in making better decisions.

What follows is the story of how Alan learns what it takes to involve others to make better decisions. He learns the ins and outs of participatory decision making from a leader famous for his wisdom and decision-making abilities: King Solomon. Undoubtedly one of the most successful leaders of his day, Solomon is renowned for the depth of his insight into the human heart, his spiritual vision, and his worldly accomplishments. In his writings, Solomon weaves together a poetic, pragmatic, and philosophical view of life in a way that offers timeless guidance to leaders facing tough decisions.

Indeed, Solomon has become an icon for wise decision making. Perhaps the most famous story about him recounts a time when two women brought before him a baby, each claiming to be the baby's mother. He ordered the baby to be cut in half, and by watching each woman's reaction to his decision, he was able to discern the real mother. His reputation as a wise decision maker was launched.

In the following pages, Solomon will guide you, through his dialogue with Alan, into the heart of participatory decision making. He reveals a system that every leader can use to wisely and effectively make better decisions by involving others in the process.

Solomon will show you that there are many decision-making styles, and each has its place. You'll learn of a continuum that stretches from Now Hear This! decisions to You Tell Me! decisions, with several stops in between. He'll teach you how to pick the most appropriate style for any decision on your To Do list. Going deeper, you'll explore the differences between compliance and commitment, the impact of time on team-based decisions, and how to achieve true consensus.

By the end of the story, you'll know that there's only one answer to our workshop participant's question How can I get my people to feel as though they're involved in the decision-making process?: Involve them.

This is a book that shows you how.

TOO MUCH "TO DO"

I T HAD BEEN A LONG, hectic week. Then again, most weeks were for Alan, a new manager with one of the larger organizations in the sprawling community of Richfield. He enjoyed his job. It was challenging, exciting, stressful, and even fun at times. When he'd been promoted to a leadership role, he'd thrown himself into the position with boyish enthusiasm, wanting to make a mark by leading his staff to extraordinary levels of performance. Since his was a key department, Alan saw this as his chance to make a real difference in the organization.

But at the moment, it was Friday afternoon, and Alan couldn't wait for the weekend and a camping trip with his family. The fall sky was a bright shade of blue. The warm evening sun cast long dramatic shadows as he cut across the lawn on his way to the train station. He looked forward to unwinding on the commute.

Alan squeezed into a seat amid the usual crowd and stretched his arms and legs. His thoughts turned to that part of his new job he found overwhelming at times—decision making. Not that he couldn't make decisions—his friends would probably describe him as quite decisive—but now that he was a manager, the questions on his mind were, To what extent should I involve my staff in these decisions? And for that matter, how?

Alan was a firm believer in the power of participative management, getting everyone involved as much as possible in the operation of the department. He'd worked for many managers in the past who'd made all the decisions and then announced them to their subordinates. That wasn't very motivating.

On the other hand, he'd also worked for managers who hardly seemed to be able to decide anything and, in what Alan saw as a transparent attempt to mask this flaw, delegated nearly every decision to the staff and called it empowerment. In that environment, decisions that should have been made quickly seemed to drag on forever, and rarely did Alan or his coworkers feel empowered. Instead, they felt paralyzed.

To pass the time, Alan took out a legal pad and began listing the various decisions on his plate at the moment. He usually found that putting things on paper helped him gain greater clarity. After a few minutes, his list looked like this:

PENDING DECISIONS

Meeting the numbers. We need a plan to make the numbers this quarter or we're in big trouble. I think I know what we need to do, but should I involve the staff anyway?

Needy client. We've got a client whose revenue production has gone way down but their demands for attention have gone up. Should we pull the plug or work harder to bring them back to former levels?

Cross-functional team. Another department wants to borrow someone for a temporary team assignment for a few weeks. Who should be selected?

New equipment. Vendors have placed new equipment in our department on a trial basis and now Purchasing wants our recommendation. Who should make it?

New hire. I've got two finalists for the opening in our department who couldn't be more different from one another. Whom should I choose?

Mission statement. With everything that's changed in the department in the past year, it's probably time to rewrite the mission statement. I don't want to do this in a vacuum, but how should I involve the team?

Client troubleshooter. We need to send someone to

troubleshoot a problem to save a client. How can I pick the best resource?

Moving pains. As if we don't have enough to do, now they're moving the department, and Facilities wants to know where we want the printers, coffee machines, conference rooms, cubicles—you name it. Who's in the best position to decide?

Dueling subordinates. Two of my staff were assigned to complete a project together, and they can't agree on how to proceed. They want me to decide for them. Should I?

Employee development. I want to set a standard for the number of hours each year my employees attend some kind of employee development activity. Should I get their input before I make up my mind?

The more Alan wrote, the more frustrated he became. On the one hand, he wanted to involve his staff in as many decisions as practical and useful, believing that people were more likely to support decisions they helped make. On the other hand, he was well aware that his staff was busy with critical deadlines every day. Pulling people together to make too many decisions wouldn't be wise and could even have a negative impact, especially on productivity.

Alan paused and began rubbing his temples. He tried to concentrate on the first decision on his list: how to make the numbers this quarter. He thought about his options.

Let's see. If we keep on doing what we're doing, there's a good chance we won't make the numbers. Not good. But I have some ideas on how to turn things around. With a bit of luck and some solid effort on the part of the team, we could meet our goals after all.

That said, I'd better remember I'm the new manager, and this team has been together for a while. I've inherited a staff with internal conflicts, a range of talent and ambition, and a variety of attitudes—positive and negative. If I impose my solution too strongly, it could backfire and produce resistance instead of commitment.

But there's not much time to do a course correction. Involving them somehow (and just how would I do that anyway?) to create an action plan to meet the numbers means using valuable time they need to meet those very goals.

So, should I decide or should we decide, or should I let them decide how it gets done? It reminds me of that expression they used in the New Manager Seminar: "Hands on as much as needed; hands off as much as possible." I'd like to be a participative manager, but it's hard to know when and where to draw the line.

Suddenly, he had another thought. *How would my own former supervisors and managers have handled this decision? What would they have done?*

The notion of getting advice from some seasoned

pros appealed to Alan. He let his mind wander back to his first boss. A moment later, he could almost hear the deep, booming voice of Mike Sullivan, his supervisor from that long-ago summer when he worked on a factory floor earning tuition for college.

"Can't make up your mind, Einstein?" he could hear Mike laughing. "You've got to come up with a plan to make the numbers for this quarter? Is that it?

"Act like a manager, my boy!" Mike laughed. "What's the problem here, lad? You've got the ideas on how to fix the problem, so fix it! You're the boss, Alan. You can't be gettin' their input on every decision. You'll be wastin' their time and yours!"

Alan actually started to nod his head, when he could have sworn he heard a different voice, which he quickly remembered belonged to Linda Parks, his supervisor when he worked at the bank.

"Hold on a second," he heard her saying. "It's an important decision, perhaps, but just as important is whether your people should be involved in creating that plan. There's a good chance they know things you don't know, have information you haven't seen. How would you know you were truly prepared to create a credible action plan if you didn't at least ask them for suggestions before you made up your mind?"

Linda had a point. Of course, it was contrary to Mike's opinion, but then again, that was predictable. He remembered Mike as the kind of boss whose favorite expression might have been "When I want your opinion, I'll give it to you!"

Hmmm, thought Alan, Mike would simply decide, but Linda would get their ideas first, before making up her mind.

As if on cue, Alan heard yet another voice, that of Owen Meredith, his former football coach. Alan could almost feel Owen's arm around his shoulder as he spoke: "In my opinion, my friend, on this one they're both wrong. If you're going to be an effective leader, you've got to learn to delegate. Decisions like this, which are all about your staff and, in the best sense, their perfor- mance, belong to them. I'd put it to them like this: 'We have six weeks to make the numbers. You are the people who will do whatever it takes to do that. So, tell me what you want. Work it out among yourselves, and let me know.' I'd let the group decide. In this case, that's the best way I know of creating a realistic plan while improving morale and loyalty at the same time."

Alan sighed. He gave Owen's input a lot of weight. Playing for him had been one of the highlights of his academic years, and he knew that Owen's own staff of assistant coaches was fiercely loyal to him. Perhaps this was why.

Alan shook his head. All three of these options made sense. But obviously, he couldn't use all three.

I can see Mike's point about just making the decision quickly, and then telling the team what to do. On the other hand, it makes sense to get my team involved, one way or another. I can think of several advantages to simply delegating this decision to the team. At least for the moment, that would be one thing off my plate!

The train rolled along, and Alan put his To Do list in his briefcase. He realized that he was no closer to deciding how to make the numbers in a way that demonstrated his commitment to employee participation without surrendering his authority as a manager.

His eyes grew heavy. It had been a long week, after all. He was tired. He thought about his To Do list one last time.

"There has to be a way to know which decisions I should make myself, and which ones I should turn over to the staff," he mumbled to himself. "There has to be a way . . ." That was the last thought Alan had before he drifted off to sleep, his list still on his mind.

"There has to be a way . . ."

2

HOW TO DECIDE "HOW TO DECIDE"

A PERSISTENT TAP ON HIS shoulder snapped Alan out of a pleasant reverie. He blinked several times as his eyes readjusted to the unusual light in the train. Looking up to see who had awakened him, Alan nearly gasped.

There was a man standing in the aisle dressed in a long cotton robe. His right hand rested on Alan's shoulder. In his left, he held a long wooden pole topped with what appeared to be a bronze spearhead. He had a dark beard and penetrating eyes.

"M-m-may I help you?" Alan stammered.

"It's time to go!" the stranger replied.

"Uh huh," Alan blinked as he scanned the car. He suddenly realized that all the seats were empty. It was just him and this guy who looked like he'd just come from a toga party or a biblical clothing convention. "And you would be—"

"My name is Teman," the man answered. Moving his hand from Alan's shoulder to his elbow, Teman helped Alan to his feet and led him down the aisle with ease.

Alan walked slowly and was surprised to realize that he felt quite comfortable with this oddly dressed stranger. Perhaps it was the unexpected heat of the desert sun or maybe the pungent smell of dry, caked earth under his shoes, but the moment they stepped off the train Alan felt completely awake.

He tugged his elbow free from Teman's grip and spun back toward the train.

But it was gone.

It had been replaced by two rough-hewn, sun-weathered wooden doors that reached thirty or more feet into the sky. The doors were flanked by equally tall stone walls that seemed to stretch forever in both directions.

"W-w-what is this? Where am I?" Alan stammered.

"The palace of King Solomon," Teman answered, just as the massive doors creaked slowly open.

Alan was led through the compound to a large central building. He was surrounded by people bustling with baskets laden with fruit, flowers and other items, youngsters herding goats and cattle, and groups of well-muscled workers rolling huge stones over thick logs. Alan stared at everyone, but no one seemed to give him the slightest notice.

Once inside, Alan was struck by the silence—and by the gold. Many of the walls were covered in the precious metal, hammered into intricate designs. As they passed through a series of cool corridors, Alan's curiosity overcame his concern. This building was unlike anything he'd ever seen before.

At the threshold of a large square room, Teman stopped and motioned Alan forward. This room was more opulent than any Alan had ever seen before. The ceiling was covered in gold, and the stone walls were carved with images of pomegranates and palm leaves. In the center of the room, there appeared to be an island of pillows. Four men, dressed in starched apparel woven with golden thread, waved long fans back and forth in a slow, steady rhythm. The figure they were fanning, dressed in a shimmering robe, had his back to Alan. Without turning around, he raised his hand and gestured for Alan to join him.

As Alan cautiously circled the pillows, the figure turned, facing his guest for the first time. His eyes were blue and as luminous as crystals. He smiled and nodded for Alan to sit down.

"Welcome to my home."

Awkwardly, Alan bowed slightly. He tried to sound confident as he asked, "Who are you and where am I?"

"I am Solomon," the man answered, "and this is not just my palace, it's my school. I call it a wisdom school for leaders." Solomon stood up as he continued, his arms opening in a gesture that seemed to encompass the entire building. "It's my task to assist leaders under pressure.

"You know, Alan, the pressure you're feeling is the same pressure that every leader faces. It's the pressure to make wise decisions, which isn't easy. Making decisions is the centerpiece of your leadership practice."

Spoken like a true king, Alan thought. Oddly, he found himself trying to think of a joke to relieve the tension he was feeling. Then he wondered, How does he know I'm under pressure? For that matter, how does he know my name?

"Alan," Solomon was smiling. His unblinking eyes looked deeply into Alan's own. "We don't have time for joking. The decisions you're facing are real. The pressure you're feeling is real. The confusion you have is real. And the help I can give you is real—whether you believe I'm who I say I am or not."

For a moment, there was only the whisper of four fans moving through the still air. Given the surroundings, it was difficult for Alan to contemplate not believing this man was the genuine article—King Solomon himself.

"Okay, Solomon, let's hear your wisdom," Alan finally replied. "Let me give you a situation. I have six weeks—"

"To make the numbers," Solomon smiled as he spoke. "Yes, I know."

"How did you . . . ?" Alan stared at the bearded stranger. There was something different about him, something ancient. Not just his clothing, but also his presence. Solomon's smile—the deep lines of his face, the glow, the starlight in his eyes—all touched Alan. He found himself leaning forward, ready to listen.

"The first secret of decision making is to decide how you're going to decide," Solomon began. "Many leaders skip this step and later regret it. They start problem solving, analyzing, debating options, and brainstorming solutions with or without their staff, not even knowing how they're going to make the final decisions.

"You see, Alan," Solomon continued, "until you've decided how you are going to decide, your team won't know whether, if, or how they're going to be involved in a particular decision."

Alan jumped in, "Well, Solomon, I definitely believe in participation. I want people to participate!"

"Yes, but how do you want them to participate in the decision about making the numbers? Do you want to create a plan and let them know what it is? Or would you rather let the team make the plan, and let you know? Maybe something that's in between?

"The degree of participation that makes sense will vary from decision to decision." Solomon held up his hand, and Teman handed him what looked like a gold brush. Then he placed a stack of papyrus pages on the pillows next to Solomon.

"Remember," Solomon said, as he began to write on the first sheet, "the key is to consider how you're going to decide an issue before making that decision. Once this is done, everyone understands what the issue is, how the decision will be made, and their own role in the process.

"Not all decisions are created equally. Some should clearly be made by the leader acting alone. Others will be of higher quality if they're made with the active participation of the group and perhaps even other key individuals with a stake in the outcome.

"Wisdom," said Solomon, "comes from knowing when and how to involve others in the decision-making process. This is what I shall teach you today."

Alan shifted his posture with a sense of expectancy.

"There are five ways that leaders and teams can make decisions. The first is what I call the *Now Hear This!* style." Solomon glanced toward the doorway, where several servants appeared with trays of fruit and pitchers of water.

"That's what Mike, your supervisor in the factory, did best. He would use a *Now Hear This!* decision style if he wanted to decide what would be done to meet the numbers this quarter. Then he would explain his decision to his team. In *Now Hear This!* decisions, the leader's role is to make and announce the decision. The team's role is to listen, ask questions to be sure they understand, and implement the decision."

"I see why you call it *Now Hear This!* It may be quick and easy, as Mike says, but I have to tell you, it sounds kind of autocratic." Alan frowned, thinking of all the my-way-or-the-highway managers he'd worked for, especially early in his career.

Solomon shook his head. "Using the *Now Hear This!* style doesn't necessarily make a leader autocratic. Using it all the time might. My guess is that those managers you feel are too autocratic may be relying too much on *Now Hear This!*

"But this is a valid method of decision making that can and should be used when it makes sense. Remember, *Now Hear This!* is just one of five styles of decision making available to leaders."

"All right," Alan concurred, "I understand. But I don't think I want to use *Now Hear This!* to decide how we'll make the numbers. Not with this team. I want them to be more involved. What other choices do I have?"

Solomon stroked his chin. "Let's move on then to the next style of decision making called the *Trial Balloon*. In this approach, you'd still think through the issue before coming to the team. But instead of announcing your decision, you'd test your decision with the team."

"Excuse me?" Alan was puzzled.

"Quite simply," said Solomon, "you present your plan, clearly articulating why you think it makes sense. Then you invite the team to share their reactions, suggestions, and ideas regarding your plan. If they can convince you that an alternative is a better option, you change your mind. If not, you stick with your original choice. In either case, you reserve the authority to make the final decision."

Alan asked, "How is this really different from the first style? After all, I'm still deciding."

"Yes, Alan, you are," Solomon responded. "But notice that the team's participation has shifted from simply listening to your announcement to getting involved and giving you feedback on the implications of your decision. You would use a *Trial Balloon* when you want to ensure you've considered all the important options and used the team's insight to shape your thinking on what to do, without delegating the authority to make the final decision."

"I get it. Fascinating! What's next?"

"Next we'll take up the **Buck Stop** approach."

"**Buck Stop?**" Alan laughed. "That sounds more like Harry Truman than King Solomon."

"Exactly," Solomon laughed as well. "Harry was one of my more famous students. And indeed, he made this style famous.

"Sometimes, you don't really have enough information to make a good decision without valuable input from experts or key stakeholders beforehand. In these circumstances, you can turn to others to collect suggestions and proposals that would solve a problem, and then, either in the moment or later in the comfort of your own office, weigh the pros and cons of what you've heard and come to a decision.

"That's the process your mentor Linda did so well."

Solomon was writing on the papyrus again.

"Notice," Solomon said, "in the three decision-making styles I've just described, the leader makes the decision, either alone without any input (**Now Hear This!**), or alone before soliciting a bit of reaction (**Trial Balloon**), or alone after gathering the ideas of others (**Buck Stop**).

"There are still two other ways the decision could be made. These represent a fundamental shift in the balance of power."

Alan flinched ever so slightly in his seat. Shift the

balance of power? he thought. But I'm supposed to be in charge . . .

Solomon simply continued. "You could work with your staff to make a team-based decision together. For example, you could conduct a problem-solving meeting where alternatives are explored and the group reaches consensus on which is the best choice. That's called the *Life Raft* decision, because it's a recognition that you're all in it together."

"*Life Raft*, huh?" said Alan. "Like Captain Bligh in the movie Mutiny on the Bounty?"

"Well, it's not always that dramatic," answered Solomon. "But yes, it is a decision that affects everyone, and so everyone is given a say, including the leader.

"Finally," said Solomon, "there's one last way you can reach a decision that affects your team. As your coach Owen so often did, you could delegate the issue to the team to decide without your active participation. This is called the *You Tell Me!* style—the exact opposite of *Now Hear This!*

"With a *You Tell Me!* decision, you share with your team the issue at hand, describe the boundaries within which the decision must be made, and approve the decision they make on their own, as long as it falls within the parameters you've set.

"In your case, you could come to the team, tell them they're going to make some decisions that you will approve, explain the situation regarding the numbers, answer any questions, turn them loose, and then approve their plan once it's complete."

"I see," said Alan. He took a deep breath.

He went on. "Let me make sure I understand what you're saying. My department is in danger of not making its targets this quarter. I have five approaches available to decide how we're going to turn that around. And," Alan smiled, "how I make this decision might be as important as what the final decision is, right?"

"Exactly, Grasshopper," said Solomon, with a wink. "How is important because it determines the degree of employee participation in the decision. Clarity about how decisions will be made leads to more engaged, motivated team members."

Alan continued. "So, I can make the decision myself, and inform my staff, à la *Now Hear This!* Or I can float a *Trial Balloon* past them, just to make sure I've thought of everything before making the final decision. But if I'm thinking I'll need their input sooner rather than later, I'd ask for it up front and then make the decision —*Buck Stop* style.

"On the other hand, if I really want them to be involved and participate, I have two more choices: work with them to reach consensus—the *Life Raft* or delegate to the team the task of coming up with a solution without me—*You Tell Me!* Have I got it right?"

"You're an excellent student, Alan," said Solomon.

"Why, thank you, kind sir!" said Alan. "So, in terms of deciding how we're going to make up those numbers, obviously I should use the . . . um . . . the . . . uh . . . Wait! Which style should I use?"

"Perhaps you should freshen your beverage, Alan," said Solomon, as he produced a clean sheet of papyrus. "It's time to drill down a little deeper."

3

COMMITMENT OR COMPLIANCE

A LAN SIPPED HIS WATER AS Solomon took another sheet of papyrus. There sure is a lot to this team-based decision-making stuff, Alan thought. Life was a lot easier when I was an "individual contributor"—I never had to figure out how to approach decisions. I just made them when I could, or passed them up to my manager when I couldn't!

"So," said Solomon, breaking the silence. "Welcome to management! Remember, Mama said there'd be days like this!"

Alan laughed.

"Now that you know the five styles of team-based decision making, are you ready to go a bit deeper with your decision about coming up with a plan to meet those numbers?"

"Absolutely," Alan replied. "But can I use some of

those pages to take notes for myself?

"I'll write down everything you will need. And you can keep these notes when you leave here. It will be better if you give your full attention to our conversation.

"Now, let's talk some more about how to decide how to decide," Solomon said. "The first step in wise decision making is knowing the five styles to choose from, and the second is knowing how to choose the most appropriate style for a given situation."

"Makes sense," Alan said. "But how does one do that? It's starting to sound complicated!"

"Alan, do you remember learning how to drive a car?" Solomon asked.

"Sure! My father taught me. I hope I have his patience when I teach my own kids how to drive."

"You'll probably agree that when you first were learning to drive, you tried to keep a lot of things on your mind all at once: when to accelerate, how to grip the steering wheel, where to put your attention on the road ahead, how often to glance in the rearview mirror, and so on."

"Yes, that is so true! I found myself wondering how I'd ever drive as effortlessly as my father. I remember gripping the wheel so tightly—at the ten-and-two positions, of course."

"Learning to make high-quality decisions that

involve your team is no different from learning to drive. In the beginning, there is a lot to think about. That's why I'm here—to explain all the ins and outs of team-based decision making. But trust me. With experience, it gets a lot easier—and quicker, for that matter. Soon it will become second nature.

"Let's start with an underlying assumption," Solomon said as he began writing.

There is no "one right way" to decide an issue.
There are many variables to consider
and you must decide for yourself
*the relative importance of those **variables.***

Alan look puzzled, so Solomon took the time to elaborate. "What I'm going to offer you now are guidelines and principles, not rules. Practice and careful application of these principles will lead to higher-quality decisions and a more involved, empowered staff. You won't always choose the style someone else might choose were they in the same situation, but you will understand why you chose that style, as will your team. You'll find that clarity about the decision-making process goes a long way toward producing more authentic participation from your staff."

Alan took a moment to take a long drink from his water glass. "I'm glad you said that," he said. "So often we're led to believe that there's only one correct approach to every problem."

Solomon nodded.

After a moment, Alan asked, "So, how do I pick the most appropriate style?"

"You ask yourself three questions," said Solomon:

1. To what degree do I want my staff committed to the decision?

2. How much time is available to make the decision?

3. How accustomed is my team to making decisions together?

"Each of these questions is important, and each relates to the others.

"To understand the first question, let's start with some word association. What words or phrases come to mind when I say the word commitment?"

Alan thought for a moment. "Well, let's see. I can think of several. Want me to write them on the papyrus?"

"If you like," Solomon smiled, as he handed over the brush. Alan wrote:

COMMITMENT

•Something I believe in, something worthwhile

•Sense of ownership

•Investment

•Something that's compelling

•Doing something because I want to

- Trust
- Allegiance
- Dedication
- Loyalty
- Support

"Excellent," said Solomon. "Now play the same word game, substituting the word compliance as your prompt. What words or phrases come to mind?

Alan reflected for a moment, took a fresh sheet of papyrus and wrote:

COMPLIANCE

- Doing something because I have to
- Obey
- Adhere
- Follow
- Conform to
- Submit
- Fear
- Authority
- Rules
- Chain of command

"Compliance and commitment are the opposite ends of a continuum," Solomon said. "Perhaps the easiest way to differentiate between them in terms of decisions is this: commitment-based decisions are things we *want* to do, while compliance-based decisions are often seen as things we *have* to do. Commitment-based decisions are usually made by us, while compliance-based decisions are usually imposed on us.

"That's important, because when people do things because they want to, they usually give them their best efforts. When they do things because they have to, they often do the minimum to satisfy the requirement."

"That makes sense," said Alan. "In fact, I might have a perfect example of this. I want my employees to come to work by 8:00 a.m., and for the most part, they do. I don't think it's because they all, without exception, want to come to work at that time, but they comply because that's the rule.

"But," he continued, "I've seen people get really excited about a project they're working on. When that happens, the rules about time and attendance are irrelevant. People are here all hours of the day and night—not because they have to be, but because they want to be! They're committed. They're willing to do whatever it takes to see their project to a successful completion."

"That's exactly right, Alan," said Solomon. "Compliance-based decisions are based on the idea that, in a particular instance, you simply want your people to do what they're told. There are many such situations in organizations. Turn in your weekly report by noon on Monday. Adhere to an appropriate dress code for your industry. Use a standardized protocol for submitting proposals to potential clients.

"There is little need—indeed, it would be a waste of time and effort—to seek commitment from all employees on these issues. All you really need is their compliance. Commitment is irrelevant."

Alan nodded as he peeled a grape.

"What you want to ask yourself is, *Do I simply need their compliance or do I really need a strong commitment to this pending decision?*

"If you need commitment to a decision—because you see it as something your people need to believe in, invest in emotionally, and implement because they want to— then you must choose a style that involves them." Solomon extended his hand and Alan gave him the brush. Immersing the tip into a shallow basin of ink, he drew a diagram.

Now Hear This!

Trial Balloon

Buck Stop

Life Raft

You Tell Me!

Compliance

More participation, which leads to…

Commitment

Solomon continued, "The more you want your team's buy-in and commitment to a decision, the further to the right you must travel on the continuum," said Solomon. "Beyond that, to build a highly committed team, if you're going to err, do it on the side of increased participation."

"Let's get back to your pending real-world decision on how to achieve your quarterly objectives. You know that you can apply any of the five decision-making styles to this issue. Now you're trying to decide how to decide. And you've heard me describe the first criteria to consider: commitment. Ask yourself this question: With regard to creating a plan to reach the numbers, do you need their compliance or do you really need a strong commitment to your decision?"

"Hmm," said Alan. "I don't want any plan I might conceive to be short-sighted. Which means I want at least some involvement or participation by the staff in this decision. Clearly I need more than simple compliance. At the moment, I'm thinking I want their input, and I want it before the decision is made. But I want to be involved in the final decision."

"Very well, Alan," said Solomon. "Because you want the team's involvement before the decision is made, you're ruling out Now Hear This! or the Trial Balloon. And because you want to be directly involved in the final decision, you're ruling out You Tell Me!

"That leaves you two choices for this decision: Buck Stop or Life Raft. Perhaps you should now consider the second criteria—the time available to make the decision —to narrow your choices even further."

4

THE IMPACT OF TIME

"THE FACT IS," SAID SOLOMON, "that getting commitment—which is a function of involvement—comes at a price."

"A price?"

"Yes. The cost for employee participation is time. In almost every case, it will take more time for a group to reach a decision than it does to decide on your own, other factors being equal. That's why you'll want to bring to your group only those decisions that need their commitment as well."

Solomon turned to the papyrus again and lifted the brush. "Imagine what happens when the decision is how to trim the budget by half a million dollars, or whether to launch a new project now or wait for further enhancements, or how to respond to a serious complaint by an important client.

"I think you'd agree that you'd want your team involved in these decisions because the stakes are high. Poor decisions can be difficult to overcome or even fatal in the marketplace. Involving your team can increase the quality of the decision and the level of commitment to that decision." Solomon was underlining the words quality and commitment.

"The point is," Solomon continued, "you can have higher-quality decisions that your staff supports with enthusiasm if you're willing to pay the price—time."

"How much time?" asked Alan.

"It ranges from as long as you're willing to give it to as long as it takes," said Solomon.

Solomon continued. "When you move toward more participatory styles of decision making, you begin to navigate a landscape of complex human dynamics. You'll have to consider the interpersonal relationships within the group as well as many differences: personality differences, differences in perspective, differences in impact the decision will have within the group, and so on.

"All these variables play themselves out on the continuum of time. Common sense tells you that all other things being equal, those decisions you make by yourself will take less time to make than those decisions that require the consensus of the group." Solomon with a few flourishes augmented the original continuum:

Now Hear This!
Trial Balloon
Buck Stop
Life Raft
You Tell Me!
Compliance
More participation, leading to…
Commitment
Less
. . . . . Time . . . . .
More

"What you say makes sense, Solomon. The more I involve my staff in a decision, the longer it's likely to take, but the decision will more likely be of a higher quality."

"That's it, Alan," replied Solomon. "The price for commitment and quality is time."

"Let me see if I can apply this to my make-the-numbers decision," said Alan. "I've already ruled out the Now Hear This!, Trial Balloon, and You Tell Me!

"Between the two remaining styles, it's likely the Buck Stop would take less time than the Life Raft. The more I think about it, Solomon, the more I'm leaning toward the Buck Stop as the most appropriate choice."

"Say a little more about that."

"Well, it gets them involved. Each person has the opportunity to weigh in and influence the final decision.

However, it consumes the lesser amount of time (of the two), and, to be honest, we don't have much time to get our numbers back on track. If I use a Buck Stop, I'll get everyone's ideas, so the quality of the plan improves, but I won't be wasting extra time seeking consensus on the decision when it isn't really needed.

"Whatever I decide based on their input, I'm confident they'll support the decision. That means the Buck Stop gives me a great balance of compliance and commitment. It's perfect! I'll put the item on the agenda for my next staff meeting."

Solomon smiled.

Alan walked to a window and gazed out. Around the building, gardeners were at work pruning fruit trees and digging in the fertile soil. Further away he could see what appeared to be acres of cultivated fields. Alan realized he had been unaware of the passage of time, but when he sneaked a glance at his watch, he was surprised. It hadn't changed. There had been no passage of time since he had entered Solomon's wisdom school for leaders.

Solomon broke Alan's reverie. "Care for a caveat, my friend?" He was standing with Alan by the window.

"I beg your pardon?"

"A caveat—a footnote—an exception to the rule. Think you can handle one?" said Solomon.

"Absolutely!" Alan responded.

"Unfortunately," Solomon began, with a pensive tone in his voice, "sometimes leaders who understand that reaching consensus takes time add two little words to this phrase."

"Huh?" asked Alan.

"These managers would not just say that reaching consensus takes time. They would say, 'Reaching consensus takes too much time.'"

"Ah," said Alan, thinking about several attempts to reach consensus with his own team. "I can see why they'd say that."

"But," said Solomon, "when a leader adds too much to his mental model of the time it takes for a group to make a decision, that leader is in danger of eliminating Life Raft or You Tell Me! decisions from his or her repertoire. This reduces the range of decision-making choices by 40 percent!"

"You promised a caveat," said Alan.

"Indeed I did," replied Solomon. "Here it is: The amount of time a group needs to reach consensus depends to a great degree on the maturity of the group in terms of making decisions. That is, a group that has practiced making consensus-based decisions can do so faster than a group that has not. And that means that you can coach your team to become better at reaching consensus by moving more decisions into the Life Raft domain.

"The more you do that, the closer you move toward the day when you can take a issue, turn it over to your team as a You Tell Me! decision, give them a short amount of time to work on the issue, and watch them reach consensus with a high-quality decision in a remarkably short time.

"They will flabbergast you, I promise you."

"There's little doubt of that, Solomon," laughed Alan. "It's not that I doubt what you're saying, but—"

"But what, Alan?"

"You just don't know my team," said Alan. "Putting my team and the word consensus in the same sentence is oxymoronic." He sighed. Perhaps some of Solomon's wisdom wouldn't apply to a team like mine, Alan mused. For the first time, he felt a tinge of doubt down in his bones.

5

THE POWER OF LETTING GO

"WHAT DO YOU MEAN, 'OXYMORONIC'?" Solomon asked.

"Oh," Alan answered, "an oxymoron is an expression where two contradictory terms are combined. Like deafening silence. Or team consensus, if you're talking about my group."

"I know what the word means," Solomon rolled his eyes. "I'm Solomon, remember? I just want to hear more about your team."

"My team is not mature enough to make a *Life Raft* decision. I've tried. But whenever I try to get them to reach consensus, the conversation becomes a debate. Some people argue. A few stonewall. Others just check out. We can't even agree where to meet for lunch!" Alan groaned. "At this point, the word consensus gives me a headache. It seems easier to just make decisions myself, perhaps with a little input from them."

"If you make that choice," Solomon responded, "and many leaders do, you permanently stunt the growth of your team. They will never gain the skills or the maturity to benefit from their differences, reach consensus, and take fully committed action."

"You don't know what it's like," Alan argued. "You're a king—not a manager. I want to help my team mature, but sometimes I wonder if they ever will. It seems like they would rather argue and complain endlessly than reach consensus."

"Alan, what would you say if I told you," Solomon paused, "that your team's degree of maturity is a direct reflection of your maturity as a leader?"

"I'd say that you're suggesting that their inability to reach consensus is my fault," Alan scowled.

"This is not about fault-finding, Alan. Wisdom seeks understanding, not blame. I'm suggesting that your team is a mirror in which you can see your own degree of maturity as a leader. A team's maturity will not surpass the maturity of the leader. And a leader's maturity can be measured by his or her ability to let go. When you let go, they can grow."

"What do you mean 'let go'? I never thought leadership was about letting go."

"Few do," agreed Solomon.

"And what am I supposed to let go of anyway?" Alan demanded.

"Your belief system about power."

Alan was silent. Outside the window he noticed that the sun had begun to set. Pink and orange clouds lay in a thin band just above the horizon. The perfumed air from the garden below wafted coolly over his skin.

"I beg your pardon?" He was nearly whispering. "What is my belief system about power? And how do I change that?"

"By thinking about power in a new way," Solomon said. "It always fascinates me how most managers think about power as though it were a pie," he said, as he drew a crude circle on the papyrus. "Many leaders believe that if they're going to share their power, they have to cut off a slice of their pie. To these managers, sharing power means giving away or losing part of their power pie. They're convinced that sharing power makes them weaker."

"So the team's gain is the leader's loss?" asked Alan.

"Absolutely, if you view power as a pie that can only get smaller by sharing. But not if you think of your power as the light of a candle. Now that's a powerful metaphor, if you'll forgive the pun. When you light another's candle with your own, there is no diminishment in your own light. In fact, from your flame you can light hundreds of other candles. Wise leaders recognize that they lose nothing by empowering others, just as a candle loses no light by igniting another."

"In fact, there's more light."

"Wisely put."

Alan smiled at the acknowledgment. Then he frowned. "But what about control? When I share power, don't I run the risk of losing control? Isn't exercising and maintaining control part of my job?"

Solomon sighed. "Those who cling to control haven't yet learned how to lead. The more a leader seeks to control people and events, the more people become unmanageable and events appear unruly. The strategy of control distances you from people. They hide their opinions and avoid interaction with you. The controlling leader (and this is a real oxymoron, Alan) becomes isolated. Wise decisions rarely grow in isolation. Surely you can recall working for a controlling leader." Solomon relaxed and waited.

Alan grimaced. "One of my first bosses—I hate to even call him a leader—was controlling to the extreme. Even when he asked for input, we knew he wasn't interested. No one dared voice a counter opinion to his ideas. We all found ways to avoid him or work around him. I don't want to be—or be seen as being—like that. But after I share power and give up control, what's left?"

"Accountability." Solomon replied. "There's a difference between being in control and being accountable.

When you share power—and step with your team into the *Life Raft*—you do so for two reasons:

1. You get the depth of commitment that comes when the team helps craft its own decision, and
2. You believe that the team's combined intelligence will produce a wiser decision than one you would arrive at alone.

"But in the end, after sharing your power and letting go of your need to be in control, you're still accountable for the outcome of the decision. If the decision works out well, you share the glory with your team. But if the decision doesn't work out, you're still going to be held accountable. Sharing power doesn't reduce your accountability—it merely increases the odds that you will make better decisions. Accepting accountability is the mantle of leadership.

"But consider this for a moment. Wouldn't you rather be held accountable for decisions of higher quality to which your team is committed?"

Alan reflected for a moment. "Absolutely. That makes sense. What I'm hearing is that my team's maturity is a mirror of my own leadership maturity. As a team, they'll mature as I start to let go of control and begin to share power. And sharing power doesn't relieve me of leadership accountability, but it does make it more palatable!"

"Your heart is beginning to understand."

"So let's cut to the chase, Solomon. Once I share power and start letting go of trying to control everything, my team be able to reach consensus, right?"

"It's the first step," said Solomon. "But to reach true consensus with your team, you will all have to understand what it means to navigate a *Life Raft* decision."

6

THE CONFUSION WITH CONSENSUS

"TO MAKE A LIFE RAFT decision, you must be sure that your team has a shared understanding of what consensus is—and what it isn't," said Solomon, guiding Alan to an island of cushions. As they sat down, Solomon placed a fresh sheet of papyrus between them.

"Remember the decision your group made to change inventory tracking systems? That staff meeting dragged on an hour past the scheduled ending time."

"Oh yes, I remember that," Alan groaned. "But at least we finally got consensus!"

"You did? How do you know?" asked Solomon.

"After an hour of wrangling, Tom came up with a proposal, and I made a point to ask, 'Is everyone on board with this one?'" said Alan.

"And what did you hear in response?" said Solomon.

Alan thought for a moment. "I heard silence. I saw a

couple of heads nodding, but come to think of it, all I heard was silence."

"Which you took to mean consensus, right?"

"Right."

"You didn't have consensus, Alan. You had silence. You had a group of people who were tired and unwilling to pursue the issue further. Perhaps they all supported it, but the odds are that there were those who were simply being quiet so they wouldn't rock the boat." Solomon made two columns on the papyrus.

"Let's explore what you think consensus is."

"Well, I think it means buy-in," said Alan.

"Anything else?" asked Solomon, as he wrote down Alan's words.

"A decision I can live with. A decision I can support even if it's not exactly what I would have proposed."

"Very good. Now let's switch gears. What is consensus not?" Solomon held his brush above the papyrus.

"It's not having everyone totally satisfied with the solution?"

"Exactly. If you had that, you'd have a unanimous decision," Solomon explained. "Under those circum-stances, each person is 100 percent satisfied with the proposal. This is a rare and impractical objective for most teams and organizations. The beauty of consensus is that it is not necessary for each person to be totally satisfied."

"I can appreciate that in theory," Alan responded," but in practice, we seem to go on and on in our meetings, trying for consensus when what we're really doing is aiming at unanimity. How can I tell when everyone is satisfied enough to have reached consensus?"

"Good question. Let me offer a simple, practical technique." Solomon smiled at Alan and gave him the thumbs up sign. After a few seconds, he spoke. "Alan, what does 'thumbs up' mean to you?"

"It means okay, good, I agree—things like that," Alan answered.

"That's right." Solomon gestured vigorously. "Thumbs up is the nonverbal way of communicating complete satisfaction with an idea, solution, or proposal. If I am in total agreement with your idea, I give you my thumbs up.

"But for you and me to reach consensus, we don't have to be thumbs up. We just need to find a solution we each substantially agree with. Not 100 percent agreement—but substantial agreement. If I were to give this a number, it would mean that we each need to be at least 75 percent in agreement with the proposed solution."

Alan shook his head. "How can I measure 75 percent agreement?"

"There is no way to measure this mathematically,

Alan. I use this number to simply indicate that each person's agreement must be substantial—yet does not need to be total. Each person in the Life Raft must honestly assess his or her own level of agreement. They can't fight for 100 percent. And they can't just give up and go along or sit by silently.

"And I can indicate this substantial level of agreement to you by having my thumb horizontal, like this." Solomon slowly began to turn his thumb from pointing straight up until it was parallel with the ground.

Solomon went on. "The horizontal thumb means 'I will support' this decision. 'It's not exactly what I would have done, but it's close enough to warrant my full support.'

"On the other hand, I can also point my thumb to the ground—a position made famous by the Romans in their Coliseum when the crowd decided whether the gladiator lived or died." Solomon pointed his thumb straight down to the floor. "What does this thumbs down sign mean to you?"

"It means no, not okay, I disagree, the idea should be killed—things like that," Alan said.

"Exactly." Solomon returned his thumb to the horizontal position. "For a group to be in consensus, all must have their thumbs at least parallel to the ground. While it might be wonderful to have all thumbs point skyward, it simply isn't necessary. Consensus is achieved when there is no thumb pointing downward."

Alan held up his thumb and moved it from the horizontal position to the vertical position. "So consensus means finding a proposal that each person substantially agrees with and will fully support. And I can test for consensus by asking everyone to show their thumbs!"

"You understand consensus and the thumbs technique, Alan." Solomon smiled.

"I'm realizing two other things that consensus is not," Alan said. "It is not debate. Nor is it smoothing over differences."

"That's right," Solomon agreed, adding these to the papyrus. "Consensus is a process of uncovering differences, identifying aspirations, and exploring ideas in order to discover the wisdom of the team. Teams that fail to work creatively with differences will either get stuck in debate or settle for a compromise."

"Wait! What's wrong with compromising?"

"Compromising reflects the lowest common denominator of the team's thinking. Rarely does it express the group's wisdom, aspiration, or creativity. In compromising, team members avoid the challenge of the Life Raft."

"Add it to the list," Alan agreed.

Solomon did so, and then he held up the papyrus. "Is there anything missing?" he asked.

"I don't see voting anywhere," Alan suggested.

"Which column do you think voting goes under?"

"Well, it's not consensus. Because when a team votes, the majority rules. Minority voters may not be even close to being satisfied with the decision."

"Correct. To be sure, voting is a legitimate decision-making process, but it's not very effective at producing commitment. I see it too often used by a leader wanting to avoid making the tough call (Buck Stop) or by a team wanting to avoid the tough work of resolving their differences (Life Raft)."

Alan glanced at Solomon's chart. It looked like this:

Consensus Is . . .

Consensus Is Not . . .

Buy-in

Shared understanding

Best thinking

A decision each person "can live with"

Unanimous

Debate

Compromise

Voting

"But let me ask you something, Solomon," said Alan. "How can we ever achieve consensus when members of the team have personal agendas and preset ideas of what the outcome should be?"

7

CONDUCTING CREATIVE
CONVERSATIONS

SOLOMON DRANK FROM HIS CUP before continuing. "Helping your team reach consensus will put your leadership skills to the test. By its nature, consensus requires flexibility from everybody. Once people agree to work toward consensus, they must shift from defending their positions to seeking the best thinking they can generate as a team. And to do that, each team member must be willing to do two things."

"And those are?"

"Everyone in the *Life Raft* must be willing to *plant* their stake and they must be willing to *move* their stake."

"Excuse me?"

"Planting your stake means putting your idea on the table. It's letting people know what you think. When you plant your stake, you share your perspective, explain your reasoning, offer a proposal, and openly declare where you stand on the issue."

"I have several team members who are very willing to plant their stakes," Alan grinned. "But sometimes it seems like they've planted them in cement. It's as if once they put their ideas on the table, they become locked in. The conversation becomes a debate. Instead of thinking out loud together, we end up in a competition for who's right. In the end, there are winners and losers. But, really, the big loser is the team. After a debate-filled meeting, team morale is in the pits. The water cooler is buzzing with blame, hurt feelings, and cynicism."

"Alan, you are correct—there can be no winners and losers in the *Life Raft*. Competition and debate sink the *Life Raft* process."

Solomon touched the fingertips of one hand to those of the other.

"This kind of interaction has been going on for thousands of years," he said. "One of your responsibilities as a leader is to help your stake planters develop the second and equally important skill—the ability to move their stakes.

"Stake movers are open to learning. They see their individual ideas as simply one perspective, not necessarily the one right answer. They allow the input of others to impact their own thinking, and they eagerly adopt new proposals, ideas, and input in order to seek the best thinking available in the group.

"Alan, to get the most of the *Life Raft*, every member of your team will need to cultivate both a willingness to plant stakes and a willingness to move them.

"As you've said, some are already comfortable planting their stakes, voicing opinions, and offering ideas. But when stake planters feel threatened, they often argue, dig in, and dominate the conversation. Your role as a leader will be to coach these people so that they're able to let go of cherished ideas and embrace a new way of thinking. Coach them to understand that changing one's mind is not a sign of weakness.

"Others are more comfortable moving their stakes. When stake movers are threatened, they tend to say yes when they mean no, they avoid conflict, and often bury their best thinking to maintain group harmony. You must encourage them to speak out and risk voicing their ideas. Consensus is only achieved when people freely plant—and move—their stakes.

"Let me share a secret with you," Solomon said. Leaning toward Alan he almost whispered, "While dominating and giving in appear quite different on the outside, they are both forms of self-protection that do not allow the power of the *Life Raft* process to develop."

"What power are you talking about?"

"The power of creativity," Solomon answered. "As a

team matures and as team members drop their self-protective habits, the untapped creativity of the team emerges. Fresh insights and new ideas arise spontaneously. There is a sense of shared purpose and alignment that accelerates the consensus building."

"I know one thing for sure," Alan reflected. "Using the *Life Raft* will demand a lot of the team. And of me."

"Very true," replied Solomon. "Mastering the *Life Raft* represents major growth for leaders and teams. This way of making decisions marks a fundamental shift from leader-centered decisions to team-centered decisions.

"Because of this, the first attempts may be awkward. Everyone will typically struggle a bit. This struggle can make you, as the leader, anxious. And being anxious, you will have a tendency to assert your authority. If you let that happen, you will sink the *Life Raft*. People will begin to doubt your commitment to the consensus process. They will check out.

"Learn to feel your anxiety without having to act upon it. Discipline yourself to support the team as everyone learns how to navigate the Life Raft to the shore of consensus. It will be worth it.

"When you and your team are skilled at making *Life Raft* decisions, you will have all five decision-making styles at your disposal. When all you need is simple compliance, you'll use the **Now Hear This!** or **Trial Balloon**.

"When you need a bit of compliance, a bit of commitment, and want to make the final decision yourself, you'll use a **Buck Stop**.

"When it's clear that commitment to the decision is far more important than mere compliance, you'll invite the team into the **Life Raft**, or delegate the decision to them using the **You Tell Me!**"

"I'm ready to get started," said Alan, with fresh energy and a sense of enthusiasm about his To Do list. "And you know what, Solomon? I've changed my mind about how to reach a decision on making the numbers. I want my team involved and committed. I'm going to get everyone in the **Life Raft** together and figure this one out!"

"I understand completely, and I agree," responded Solomon. "You have learned much here today. The day grows long. Let me share with you one more teaching before you leave."

8

KNOWING HOW "TO DO"

S OLOMON GLANCED AT TEMAN AND clapped twice. The man swiftly left the room but returned in an instant. He knelt beside Alan and presented him with what appeared to be a simple wooden flute.

"Examine, the instrument, Alan," said Solomon, "and tell me what you see."

"Well, it's a flute." Alan turned the instrument in his hands. "It has five holes and a notched mouthpiece."

Solomon put out his hand and Alan gave him the flute. He raised it to his lips. Inhaling deeply, Solomon closed his eyes and began to play. He played a single note. One note that seemed to go on and on...just that note. And then silence.

"What would you say if that was all the music I could play?" Solomon asked.

"I'd hardly call it music," Alan answered. "It was just one note."

"Many leaders are like that," said Solomon. "They are stuck on one note of the decision-making scale. But, as you have learned, there are five styles of leadership decision making. Just as a master musician creates music using all five notes of the flute, so too does the mature leader develop a culture of trust, collaboration, and efficiency by using all five decision-making styles. The mature leader and team can participate in any style of decision making with equal skill and grace. In one meeting they easily shift from a *Now Here This!* decision at one point to a *Life Raft* decision at another. Understanding that different situations require different decision-making styles means they can apply the *Buck Stop* as readily as the You Tell Me! approach. And before making any decision, the mature leader always clarifies —"

"How the decision will be made," Alan interrupted, "because in doing so, everyone will understand what the issue is, how the decision will be made, and their own role in the process.

"Not only that," Alan continued, "but not all decisions are created equal—some should be made by the leader acting alone. Others will be of higher quality if they're made with the active participation of the team.

"Wisdom," concluded Alan, as he cleared his throat,

"comes from knowing when and how to involve others in the decision-making process."

Alan looked at Solomon. The king's eyes radiated with an obvious inner joy. The two men stood up and Solomon placed his hand on Alan's shoulder.

"Welcome to a new world of leadership," his voice resounded from the carved walls, "one that will be as rewarding as it is challenging. Wherever you go, remember that the wisdom you need is always close at hand. In fact, it is within you. As you face difficult decisions, recall our time together. Remember what you have learned. But, most of all, remember that you can return to this wisdom school at any time. Simply open yourself to the wisdom within."

Solomon squeezed Alan's shoulder and closed his eyes in concentration.

Alan followed suit, closing his eyes and listening within.

He felt the hand squeeze again, and then it began to shake him gently. Alan opened his eyes.

The train conductor was leaning over him. "Sir, we're coming to your stop."

Alan struggled to focus on what he was hearing. *Stop? Who is this guy with the blue cap shaking his shoulder? Where's Solomon?*

"Your stop, Sir. Ocean View Boulevard," the trainman repeated as he turned away.

Alan looked out the window. The train was pulling into the station. It was twilight and the silhouettes of telephone poles flashed across the window. He heard the brakes screech. And then the gradual slowing until the train lurched to a standstill. Alan stood up grabbing his briefcase and newspaper. He felt a bit dazed as he fell into line behind the other disembarking passengers.

On the platform, Alan paused. *What had just happened? Was it a dream?*

"Dad!" a voice yelled over the crowd. It was his youngest son, Denny. He was hanging out of the window of the van, waving Alan over.

Alan took a deep breath to clear his head and made his way to the van.

"Hi honey," his wife, Judith, leaned over for a kiss. "We have some things to decide. I know we were planning to go camping this weekend."

"Hi, sweetie! That's true. I'm really looking forward to it. Has something changed?" Alan crawled into the passenger seat.

"Well, the kids have some different ideas."

"Dad, this is the last real beach weekend before the water gets too cold," Sarah explained. "Everyone in my class is going to be at this big cookout."

"Uh-huh."

"And you know, Dad," Denny chimed in, "there were these coupons for discounts to the ballgame in the paper. So we could go to the game while they go to the beach."

"Is that everything?" Alan raised an eyebrow.

"Not quite," Judith said. "My folks called up and they're going to be in the area on Saturday. So I thought we could have them over for a barbecue."

"Camping in the desert is sounding better and better to me," Alan pretended to whine.

"Dad!!" Sarah's voice cut through the van.

"Alan," Judith was staring at him. "What's that in your hand?"

"The newspaper. Why are you looking at me like that?"

"That's not a newspaper."

Alan looked down. In his left hand he held a sheaf of papyrus sheets tied together with a strip of rawhide. Alan undid the knot. As he stared at the papyrus, the image of a man named Solomon flashed across his mind.

"Well, you see," he began, "these are some notes from a sort of wisdom school I attended today. And you know what? I think they'll be able to help us make a wise decision about what to do this weekend. In fact, I'm sure of it."

A LAN RETURNED TO WORK MONDAY morning, refreshed from a relaxing weekend with his family and eager to apply the wisdom of Solomon to his To Do list. He closed his office door, pulled out the list, and went to work. After thirty minutes or so, he had decided how to decide the most important items on his list.

Alan's list is typical of the decisions facing leaders in organizations everywhere. If you haven't had something similar to each of these items on your own To Do list yet, you probably will. In our workshops across the country, we've asked managers and supervisors to apply the wisdom of Solomon to each of these issues, presented in the form of miniature case studies. Now it's your turn to decide how to decide.

What follows are ten situations requiring a decision.

Your challenge is to determine how you would involve your staff in each of those decisions. After each scenario, you'll find a place to record the decision-making style you would select if this situation were yours to handle and some room for brief notes on why you would use that style.

Next, you can compare your response with Solomon's choice, which is the style most frequently chosen by participants in our workshops after having learned the decision-making continuum and the factors that determine which style to choose.

Ready?

1. The Case of the Client on "Life Support"

Your department has a long-term relationship with a client we'll call Needy Client Incorporated, or NCI. Formerly one of your best customers, the revenue this client delivers to your organization has steadily declined, while its demands for attention have risen. At this point, it's clear that your team is spending more resources on NCI than any other client who produces similar revenue. You've begun to wonder, Should we pull the plug on NCI, or spend even more time and effort to try bringing NCI revenues back to previous levels?

Which style would you choose?

Why?

2. The Case of the Cross-Functional Team Assignment

Another department wants to borrow someone from your staff for a temporary cross-functional team assignment on a part-time basis for about six weeks. You're willing to help out, but the question is, Who gets the nod?

Which style would you choose?
Why?

3. The Case of the Office Equipment Upgrade

Several office supply vendors have placed equipment in your department on trial over the past three months for a hands-on review. What you've been using is hopelessly out of date, and it's time for more efficient tools. The Purchasing Department is awaiting your decision on which vendor you'd recommend.

Which style would you choose?
Why?

4. The Case of the Competing New Hires

There's a vacancy in your department, and you've

been interviewing for some time. You've narrowed down the list of candidates to two finalists, who are about equal in your eyes, even though they're quite different from one another. How would you decide to which candidate to make an offer?

Which style would you choose?

Why?

5. The Case of the New Mission Statement

You've been managing the department for a while, and you've been thinking that it's time to rewrite the department's mission statement, because so many things have changed since it was created. The department has new responsibilities and a different reporting relationship since a recent reorganization. Without a doubt, you want input from the team—but in what form?

Which style would you choose?

Why?

6. The Case of the Client Troubleshooter

Sooner or later, it happens to everyone. One of your customers is complaining of poor service—and they're probably right. Trouble is, the fix isn't going to be easy. You'll need to send someone from your department to the client to troubleshoot the problem and come back with a solid recommendation to fix it and retain the client's business. How do you decide whom to send?

Which style would you choose?

Why?

7. The Case of the "Meeting the Numbers" Plan

This quarter hasn't started out with a bang. Fact is, halfway through, your department is waaaay behind the numbers. You've got some definite ideas on a plan to make up the difference in the next six weeks. Should you trust your gut and go with them—or involve your staff in some way in creating a plan?

Which style would you choose?

Why?

8. The Case of the Department Move

As if there wasn't enough to do, now they're moving your department to another building. The arrangements for cubicles, printers, the coffee machine—you name it —need to be determined. Of course the organization has some guidelines, but it's up to each department head to submit a plan detailing what and who should go where. How would you make those decisions?

Which style would you choose?

Why?

. . .

9. The Case of the Conflicting Subordinates

Two members of your staff have been assigned to work together on an important project, but they can't come to an agreement on the best way to proceed. They want you to decide for them. Each has come to you independently and made a case for his or her action plan, and both await your decision.

Which style would you choose?

Why?

10. The Case of the Employee Development Standard

In your opinion, ongoing employee development is very important, and you want everyone on the team to take advantage of the many opportunities for professional growth that are available, both within and outside the organization. You want to set an expectation that each employee will attend X number of hours in some kind of developmental activity. How should you decide what that number will be?

Which style would you choose?

Why?

THE WISDOM OF SOLOMON

. . .

Here's the style that Solomon would recommend for each of the preceding cases.

1. The Case of the Client on "Life Support":
  Life Raft

This is a decision for which you'll want all the brain power you can muster—and all the commitment. It's possible that some of your teammates have more information about this client than do you. Get everyone in the Life Raft and get consensus on whether to pull the plug or redouble the effort.

2. The Case of the Cross-Functional Team Assignment:
  Trial Balloon

As the manager, you're the "director of player personnel." Review your players, make your choice, but run it by the team in case the person you choose has a priority you haven't considered to keep him or her from joining the cross-functional team.

3. The Case of the Office Equipment Upgrade: *You Tell Me!*

Your people have been using the equipment and know far better than you what's working and what isn't. Delegate this one and get it off your plate.

4. The Case of the Competing New Hires: *Buck Stop*

Many managers now make a practice of having all finalists for a position interview (or at least meet) with every member of the staff. They can often get information that will tip the balance one way or the other, plus give you a heads-up about the chemistry and potential fit of someone who looks good on paper, and even interviews well, but may still not be right for the team. The final decision is yours.

5. The Case of the New Mission Statement:

Buck Stop

This one is tricky, and many leaders make a fairly persuasive case for the Life Raft. After all, they want their teams fully committed to a mission statement. However, a Buck Stop approach would get every team member's input and yet reserve for the manager the ultimate act of leadership—that is, the final say in terms of clarifying the team's purpose.

6. The Case of the Client Troubleshooter:
   Now Hear This!

A decision that seems to require compliance, not commitment. You should know your staff well enough to pick the most appropriate person for this assignment.

7. The Case of the "Meeting the Numbers" Plan:
   Life Raft

Time to gather the troops in the conference room and

hunker down until the group has hammered out a plan —a plan they're committed to follow.

8. The Case of the Department Move:
Trial Balloon

At the end of the day, deciding who and what goes where and when after a department move may be the most challenging decision you'll ever face! People attach a lot of meaning to their workspaces. Follow the organizational guidelines and run it by your team before submitting the plan, just in case someone has some input that makes you change your mind. An argument is occasionally made that this should be a Buck Stop decision, primarily when you need more information before creating a straw plan.

9. The Case of the Conflicting Subordinates:
You Tell Me!

This is a great coaching opportunity for the leader. If you make the mistake of resolving this issue for these employees, you'll be teaching them to come to you to resolve future differences—not work it out themselves. Think of it this way: they're bringing you a monkey and trying to place it on your back. Don't take the bait. Hear them out, but leave the decision on how to proceed in their capable hands, where it belongs.

10. The Case of the Employee Development Standard: *Now Hear This!*

One of your most important responsibilities as a leader is to set the standards and expectations. Only you can decide what you stand for.

ACKNOWLEDGMENTS

From Gary:

I learned about collaborating on a book back in the fifth grade, when my friend Bob Eats and I co-authored *The Super Scientist and the Time Machine*, an effort at science fiction that featured – what else? – two fifth grade boys who help a scientist pilot his time machine back to the days of the dinosaurs. Never published – thank goodness! – it nonetheless gave me the taste for writing and for working on big projects with others.

This has been a labor of love. I first want to thank my writing partner, Eric Klein, who brings a gentle spirit and deep wisdom to the work. Our careers have crossed paths many times over the past twenty years, and I've always been enriched by our relationship.

There have been many others who've encouraged me

along the way. Dr. Trudy Sopp – thanks for your unconditional support. Dr. Keren Stashower, Kim Piker, Robin Reid – you've each touched my heart and mind indelibly. Ann Marie Stuart – you were the best business partner in the world. John Gavaras – you have the gift of laughter, and I treasure you for that.

Most of all, I want to thank my beautiful daughters, Lyndsey and Hallie, who are becoming incredible women right in front of me. Where the time has gone, I cannot say, but it would be impossible to me more proud of you. Thank you, girls, for putting up with Dad all this time and forgiving him his parental mistakes. As you know, and once and for all, you're *both* my favorite!

From Eric:

The first time I jumped off a mountain was on a business trip to Alaska. The paragliding instructor told me to run as hard as I could toward the cliff edge. Feeling doubt and excitement, I ran.

I jumped … and floated on the wind surrounded by mountains glowing in the setting sun.

Writing a book is like jumping off a cliff. When taking this creative leap into the unknown, it helps to have a partner. I am blessed to have had Gary Winters as a partner in this adventure. Gary is one of those rare people who fuse brilliant creativity with focused practicality.

My understanding and practice of leadership has been shaped by many people over the years. Paramount is my spiritual mentor, Goswami Kriyananda – your teachings come to life every day. Bob Anderson's genius for modeling the deeper dimensions of leadership inspire my best work – thanks for your friendship. Thank you to Blake Anderson, Dana Smith, Denny Stone, Nancy DickersOn-Hazard, and Joan Waltman – clients who have become friends and mentors.

Writing while running a business would not have happened without Carol Emerson – queen of the hard copy, and mystic project manager.

Thank you to Deborah, Aaron, and Nathanial for being such radiant examples of spirit-in-action, and for keeping your humor and perspective when I lose mine. I love you.

From Gary & Eric:

This book would not exist without the support, efforts, genius, and skills of the following people:

Freya Reeves – you made it happen by keeping the big picture while lovingly caring for each word. Thank you for bringing grace, thoughtfulness, and spark to the process.

Lynn Fleschutz – your artistry and diligence have raised the level of our work. Thank you for making us look good.

Denny Stone – your attention to detail made a huge difference. Thank you for asking questions.

About Gary:

I got off to a slow start...

When I was a child, my best friend loved taking things apart, just to see how they worked. His passion was anything mechanical – cars, toy trains, woodworking. Somehow, he knew from the get-go what how he would spend his life. He became a mechanical engineer.

By comparison, I never quite knew what I wanted to be as I was growing up. I loved playing baseball (and often imagined myself as the pitcher in the ninth inning of game seven of a World Series), and a wide variety of school assignments: drawing dinosaurs for my Earth Science class, creating a bug collection for my Biology class, and getting the lead role (made famous by both Spencer Tracy and Steve Martin) in our high school production of *Father of the Bride*.

Off to college, where I majored in English, before switching to Speech Communications, before settling on Psychology. I discovered a passion – understanding how *people* tick. I graduated with a Master's in counseling psychology with *no* marketable job skills. I stumbled through a few false starts in sales and advertising before my epiphany. Taking a class in "consulting skills," I learned there were people who made their living combining psychology and business. At the time, it was the dawn of the field of Organization Development.

I hitched my wagon to an OD consultant who was kind enough to take me under his wings and show me the way. A few years later, with a new skillset, I made the decision to become an independent, free-lance management/OD consultant. That was thirty years ago, and I've never looked back. I've been blessed with great opportunities, great projects, and *lots* of variety.

But it all worked out in the end...

I've been able to work with organizational leaders around North America. From a giant project with the first American super-collider project, to high-tech start-ups, from Apple in the days of System 7 to IBM as it rolled out the ThinkPad, plus a broad variety of government organizations at the city, county, state, and national level.

I've worked with small organizations with less than a dozen employees, family-owned businesses, cities with over 10,000 employees, manufacturing plants with 20,000 employees, major hospitals and other organizations going through reorganization, and many more.

To have had the chance to rub elbows with all kinds of leaders, from the small cross-functional team leaders to CEOs, from front-line supervisors to General Managers, from those in the public sector to those in the private sector, has been a thrill and a blessing.

Throughout it all, I was able to get "under the hood" and see what the most effective among them actually did. What made them tick. *It became my passion to learn from them and teach it to others.*

To date, I have consulted to over 300 organizations. I am past president of the Organization Development Network of San Diego and a former director of the Management Development Center at San Diego State University.

I launched **The Leadership Almanac** in 2008, a blog which explores the practical side of leadership. Today you can explore a rich collection of over 120 free articles ranging from how leaders create a compelling vision to how they sweat the small stuff, from how they make tough decisions to how they navigate a difficult conversation, from how they inspire to what makes them perspire.

Today, I specialize in **coaching** leaders one-to-one (from front-line supervisors to CEOs), **writing** highly practical books on management, and **facilitating** leadership seminars, workshops, and retreats (with over 40,000 participants in groups of 25-30 to date). I've published seven books for managers and created the immensely popular **S.T.A.R.T.** (Supervisors Transition & Readiness Training) program, which has helped over 1,250 participants prepare for their careers in management.

While I live in Reno, Nevada, far from my Ohio roots, I work with clients throughout the United States. In my free time, I enjoy woodworking, photography, riding a recumbent trike, and making music (a keyboardist by training, I'm taking on the mountain dulcimer).

I can be reached at (619) 840-0148 or by email at gary@garywinters.com.

About Eric:

I grew up in New York City

But, my summers were spent at a place called Fire Island – a narrow spit of sand lying between the Great

South Bay and the Atlantic Ocean. That's where I first learned about turning "big ideas" into reality.

My big idea, back then, was to put on *Fire Island's 1st Kid-run Carnival*. It took my friends and me two weeks to prepare the games, contests, and carnival rides. We stapled posters advertising the *Kid-run Carnival* on all the telephone poles within biking distance.

It was a huge success. We were overrun with customers. *The Fire Island News* came and took photos and interviewed me about the "big idea".

The *Kid-run Carnival* taught me that if you have a *big idea* and pursue it with focus and discipline, you can make it real.

Since 1989, I've helped over 18,000 people bring *big ideas* to life in their work

I've worked in a wide variety of settings: Fortune

500 companies, healthcare, municipal, governmental and non-profit organizations as well as mid-size companies. I've worked with individuals and teams. They've been corporate executives, middle managers, nurses, engineers, mayors, city planners, and factory workers.

I've found that every person wants to contribute, to create, and to grow

Everyone has this urge to contribute in ways that matter. It's part of our human nature. People, in every department and discipline, want to invest themselves in big ideas. They want to be part of something that matters.

By working with thousands of clients I've learned a lot about human motivation and how to focus it so people become *more engaged, more accountable, and more innovative* at work.

I combine my real-world experience with extensive study & meditation

I'm a passionate student of human development, leadership, and spiritual traditions. I read at least 100 books a year – in these areas, primarily. I've had a meditation practice for 40 years. (And I've taught meditation for 25 years).

It's this combination of real-world experience, with deep study and meditation, that has led to the unique approach I call – Resistance*Free* Change.

What I've discovered is that change doesn't have to be a struggle.

Change can be resistance-*free*. If you connect with the deep drives for *growth, learning, and making a difference* that motivates human behavior.

I'm sure that growing up in a family of entrepreneurs & artists biases me towards seeing people as fundamentally creative. As a child, I saw adults pursuing big ideas in business and the arts.

My maternal grandparents came to this country as immigrants and built a prosperous fashion company in the garment district of New York City. My father dropped out of dentistry school to be an entrepreneur. My mother was a painter.

I was taught at an early age that success comes from blending creativity and discipline.

I was taught to question the status quo and to keep improving my skills by *learning something new every day.*

The Resistance*Free* Change system is not static. It keeps evolving and deepening.

Through interaction with clients (as well as continuous learning) our programs have become both *simpler and more powerful.*

In addition to working with thousands of people, my work has been featured on CNN and in the LA Times, HealthCare Forum, The American Medical Journal, Leadership Reflections, Quality and Productivity, and the Association Management Magazine.

My most recent program is *You are the Leader You've Been Waiting For*

It's based on my book, of the same title, which won a 2008 Nautilus Book Award for being a world-changing book promoting positive social change and responsible leadership.

I'm also the co-author of the best selling book *Awakening Corporate Soul: Four Paths to Unleash the Power of People at Work* (over 250,000 copies sold) and *To Do or Not To Do: How Successful Leaders Make Better Decisions* based on research and experiences with more than 200 companies.

I live by the ocean

My wife, Deborah, and I have two wonderful sons – Nathaniel (www.nathanielklein.com) and Aaron. The boys are out of the house (most of the time). We live a 5 minute walk from the Pacific Ocean in Encinitas, California (a classic Southern California beach town in San Diego's North County).

Our town is mentioned in the Beach Boys song *Surfin' USA!* Encinitas is a laid-back surfer paradise and home to the world's largest poinsettia farm. Our two sons, Nathaniel and Aaron are both surfer dudes.

Deborah and I enjoy walking on the beach, playing in the ocean, teaching meditation, and creating our own peaceful oasis at home.

Please feel free to call (760) 436-5535 or email me – eric@dharmaconsulting.com – with any questions. I would love to hear about the big idea that's inspiring you.

ALSO BY ERIC KLEIN

Awakening Corporate Soul

You Are the Leader You've Been Waiting For